TRATTLERHOF
★★★★

THE TRATTLERHOF

AND ITS HISTORY • THE CHRONICLE OF THE HOUSE

Publisher
Jakob V. Forstnig

The Trattlerhof and its History
The Chronicle of the House

Publisher: Jakob V. Forstnig, Hotel Trattlerhof
Based on the detailed chronicle from the Carinthian Provincial Archive

Layout: Maria Hochmeister
Manufactured and published by:
BoD - Books on Demand, Norderstedt, Deutschland

In our Jubilee year 2012 we are pleased
to present the eventful history of our house
to our guests, and we hope you will enjoy
reading this chronicle!

Jakob V. Forstnig
Hotel Trattlerhof

From times gone by and the way it was then,
to the here and now, this year!

THE CHRONOLOGICAL HISTORY
OF THE "TRATTLERHOF" AND
ITS INHABITANTS

Bad Kleinkirchheim in the 1960s

1166 Like many areas in the Alpine region, the Benedictine monks allowed the valley to be cleared and systematically settled. "Kirchheim" was first mentioned in 1166. The town remained under the governance of Millstatt until the abolition of the monastery in 1773, and following this until the abolition of the landlord system in 1848. (From the 16th century onwards the town is referred to as "Kleinkirchheim" to prevent confusion with the mining community of Großkirchheim.)

1469 The Order of St George took over the monastery. One year later, in 1470, the first rental roll of Kirchheim was drawn up (= the tax register of the Order's rural subjects). At this time the "Trattler" was not yet listed.

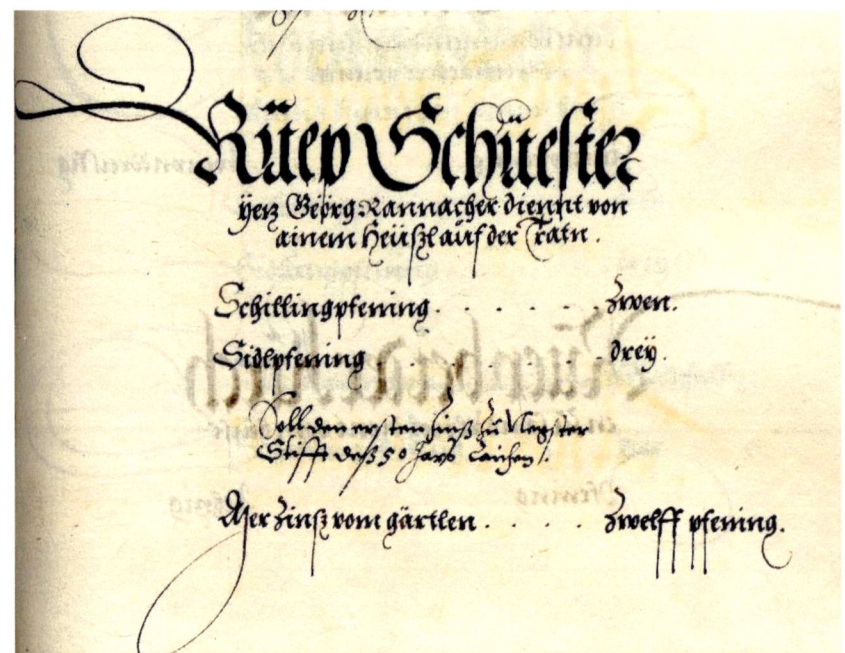

The payment of interest on a debt by Ruep Schuster was recorded in the record of taxes (1520) for a small house (Häusel) on the Tratten.

FIRST MENTION

1520 The tax records of the Knights of St George in Millstatt dating from 1520 recorded a Ruep Schuster, who paid tax on a small house on the Tratten. The rental roll records a number of such "small houses" in Untertschern. Small chalets which did not possess much land sprang up here between 1470 and 1520. Their occupants derived their income from crafts and petty trade, as indicated by the family names recorded at the time, such as Kirschner (cherry grower), Schuster (shoemaker), Schneider (tailor) and Kramer (merchant). These properties continue to be described as *"Häusel"* (small houses) up to the end of the 16th century, and only later are they called *"Kheuschen"* (cottages).

1585   Until this time the property was owned by the Rannacher family.

ALREADY AN INN BY THIS TIME

1585   The Rottenstainer family (= from the small village of Rottenstein near Kleinkirchheim) became the owners. In view of the building's position on the much travelled road, we can assume that the inn trade was already being practised here in 1592.

1598   The Jesuits took control of Millstatt.
Times got harder for the inhabitants, their taxes went up and inheritance law became more arbitrary.

1639   Veith Rottenstainer took over the Rottenstainer cottages in the lower Tschern in "Klein Kürchhamb" from his guardian Nicl Hinteregger.

Reproduction of a stone brewery from the period around 1900

57 YEARS LATER IT ALREADY HAD ITS OWN BEER AND BREAD

1642 Veith and his bride Eva Kren were awarded a series of trading licences by the Jesuits: they were granted the right to weave and trade in wool and linen fabrics, and also the right to serve food and drinks, the so-called "Tafernrecht", the right to brew stone beer, bake bread and exercise the weaver's trade. Their right to sell linen and loden cloth was thus confirmed.

Stone beer was relatively simple to manufacture. Fermentation was induced in large barrels by the use

of hot stones. Beer had been produced in this way
since the Middle Ages, and was the usual drink of
the bulk of the population in particular.

NO INHERITANCE RIGHT FOR DAUGHTERS

1688 – 1724   Andre Rottenstainer ran the "Rottenstainer or Trättler cottages" for 41 years. His daughter Maria Lassnitzer found herself unable to take them over due to the high debts of 100 guilders and the costs involved (in reality it would have entailed buying them for 200 guilders, since the tenancy right in respect of the inn did not permit it to be handed over directly to his married daughter). She suggested her "closest friend" (blood relative), her cousin Kaspar im Kray (Grayer) as the successor for the ownership of the "Trätler inn" from 1729 – 1748.

THE START OF HARD TIMES

When the Jesuits took control of Millstatt, this brought with it a period of ever increasing burdens to the farmers here. The monks pushed their subjects to the limits of what they could bear, although they always remained within the framework of what was permitted by law.

They utilised all their rights to the full, and exploited the laws of succession and tenancy to their full effect. When there was no male successor, property returned to the land owners. To some extent they even tried to remove the inheritance rights of sons. If an heir was under age and a guardian was used, the Jesuits demanded that a tribute be paid by both the ward and the guardian, in other words twice the fee had to be paid for transferring the estate (as was also the case with the Trättler inn!).

SUBSTANTIAL COMPLAINTS BY THE SUBJECTS IN MILLSTATT

1. Since time immemorial, the subjects had been obliged to supply a so-called "farm ox" weighing 2 1/2 hundredweight once a week. After this amount of meat

The land owner's seat, the Jesuit residence in Millstatt,
Valvasor around 1680

apparently became too much for the monastery
kitchen, the subjects had to pay six guilders every
other week instead of the ox.

2. The toll charges at cattle markets and the fees for
   stands at the cattle markets seemed much too high
   to the farmers.

3. The Imperial *"Fleischtaz"* (a tax on the slaughter of animals) was not adjusted in accordance with the resolutions of the Landtag (regional parliament). In Millstatt, 1 guilder and 18 kreuzer was levied for each farm which was much too high.

4. The cereal tithe levied by the Jesuits was higher than normal and their subjects complained about this.

5. Instead of the usual 11 – 13 cords of wood, the Jesuits demanded 16 cords of firewood from every farm.

6. The *"Specktaz"* (tax) that was common in the region was also increased and the subjects demanded that it be brought in line with the prescribed level of tax.

MANY COMPLAINTS TO NO AVAIL

1728 When Emperor Karl VI paid a ceremonial visit to the region in 1728, his subjects in Millstatt presented him with a *"Beschwerdelibell"*, an initial list of their complaints requesting that he remedy the unjust demands made of them by their rulers. Further endeavours (also fruitless) followed in 1730.

1735 A further memorandum with various points of complaint was handed to the Governor of Carinthia. Despite the fact that yet again investigations were ordered by the State and carried out, no agreement could be reached.

A RENEWED ATTEMPT

1736 Whilst some of the administrative offices in Millstatt did indeed reach compromises with the Jesuits in 1736, this was apparently not the case for the administrative office in Kleinkirchheim. The farmers therefore had a new memorandum drawn up for them by the Klagenfurt lawyer, Dr Plasge.

The farmers met in the Prenn guesthouse in the Afritzergraben (run by Kaspar Grayer's father-in-law) and Plasge called on them to compile precise charges against the Jesuits.

A RASCAL GETS INVOLVED

1737 The situation became increasingly confused, and in 1737 a delegation was sent to Vienna to hand in a complaint to the court of the Emperor. The farmers' representatives fell into the hands of the alleged lawyer Paul Zopf. This proved fatal for the farmers, who had acted correctly until then. Paul Zopf stirred the farmers up and all Dr Plasge's attempts at conciliation came to nothing. Paul Zopf claimed to be the Emperor's commissar and showed the farmers a forged Imperial patent which allegedly allowed them to plunder the Jesuits' residence.

FATE TAKES ITS COURSE

On 2 November 1737, there was a public rebellion. Around 300 farmers armed with sticks and muskets attacked the premises of the monastery and took the Father Superior, the Court judge and all the Jesuits they could get hold of, prisoner. However, most of them succeeded in fleeing to Spittal and

into the protection of Prince Porcia. The next day
the plundering began. The farmers stole everything
they could lay their hands on, and some of them lit
fires. The ringleader Paul Zopf managed to steal
3,000 guilders, whereupon he fled.

THE FRAUDSTER IS ARRESTED

Paul Zopf was recognised when he was resting
at the present day Trattlerhof in Untertschern.
Kaspar Grayer, the Trattler landlord at the time,
had not been amongst the rebellious farmers.
However, he arranged for his neighbour to inform
the local magistrate. Hans Trättnig, the landlord's
neighbour, hurried to the local magistrate who
arrested Paul Zopf immediately.

Hans Trättnig, who had himself played a major part
in the uprising, returned the goods he had stolen.
As he had actively repented and had delivered Zopf to
the authorities he was pardoned, and unlike the other
participants, he emerged unpunished.

The picture in the Zopfstube is a reminder of the incidents in 1737.

A later owner of the inn had this incident recorded as a painting on the wall of the inn. During renovations in the 20th century this was moved to the newly created Zopfstube.

1748 – 1751   After the death of Kaspar Grayer, Christian Wieser took over as the guardian of Jakob Grayer, who was still a minor.

1751 – 1757   Jakob Grayer owns the inn.

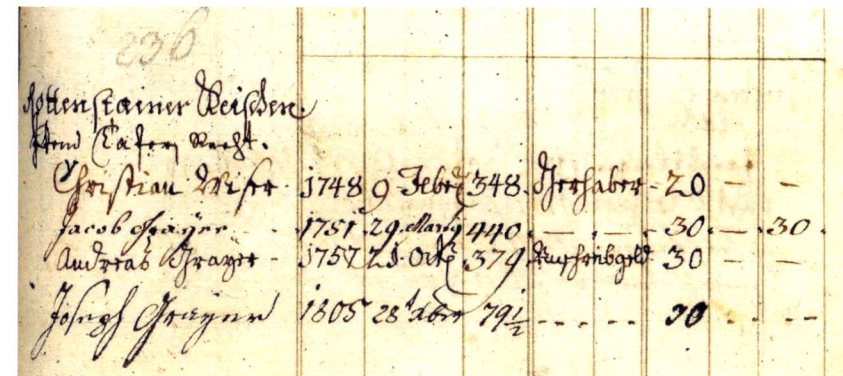

Handovers
of ownership
1748 – 1805

NOW WINE IS SERVED TOO

1757 – 1805   Ownership passes to Andreas Grayer. The Trattler inn was supplied with wine directly by a pack mule driver from the Gail Valley, who delivered the remarkable quantity of around 1,500 litres in six months!

1805 – ?   Joseph Grayer takes ownership.

1810   Then came Ignaz Grayer, known as Mall, who bought the inn back from Gertraud Hofferin in 1810 (no legal documents exist from the French administration of Upper Carinthia between 1809 and 1813).

A FINE FARM BUILT OF WOOD

1821–1843   Christian Laßnig: During his ownership, Emperor Franz I (1826 – 1829) had every parcel of land in Carinthia measured accurately. For this reason we refer to the *Franciscan land tax cadastral register* which was measured using the fathom scale (1:2880).

Franciscan cadastral register of the cadastral municipality of Kleinkirchheim around 1839, Untertschern section

At that time, the buildings of the Trattler inn were mainly constructed of wood. There is a note in the description included in the cadastral register that only two houses in Kleinkirchheim at this time had been built of stone.

THE FIRST FORSTNIG AT THE TRATTLERHOF, INITIALLY STILL IN THE "WELLNESS WING"

1840   The Forstnig family first came into contact with the landlord of the Trattler in 1840. The carpenter, Jakob I Forstnig, lived in the bathhouse *("Badstubn")* belonging to the Trattler inn.

1843 – 1847   On 6 March 1847, Jakob I Forstnig concluded an agreement with the owner Jakob Glinzer which secured a lifelong right of residence for himself, his wife Elisabeth and their two children Jakob II and Maria.

1847 – 1849   During his ownership period the agrarian landlord reform took place (1848), making him the first real owner of the property.

1849–1854   Michael Hofer acquired the property on 21 November 1849, and its value was estimated to be 1,000 guilders. This increase in value was due to the fact that Hofer was able to take possession as an actual owner, which meant that both the land and the property on it were valued.

1854–1856   Katharina Lechner, Michael Hofer's widow, later married Matthias Stampfer.

1856–1874   Matthias Stampfer inherited the inn after the death of his wife, and was recorded in the land register on 21st August 1856. His period of ownership can be regarded as thoroughly positive. During his time there were repeated purchases, so that the ground area of the estate increased.

THE TRATTLERHOF AS A CENTRE

Matthias Stampfer was also Mayor of the municipality of Kleinkirchheim from 1862 to 1879.

The Trattler inn
around 1890

During this time the mayoral office was at the
Trattlerhof. He died on 5th October 1872 and the
Trattler inn passed to his son Albin.

1874-1884 Albin Stampfer became the successor in ownership
after his father in accordance with the settlement
of the estate and the certificate of inheritance
issued on 31st December 1873. He remained the
owner for the next ten years, until he sold it in 1884
to the Forstnig family.

Vertrag,

Zwischen Jacob Glützner Besitzer dem eigenthümlichen
zur Gerichtsherrschaft Millstatt dienstbaren Trattlern
weinbehausung Urb: N° 236 Haus N° 8 zu Obermillstatt
in Kleinkirchheim Einer, dann dem Jacob Harstnig und
dessen Eheweib Elisabeth gebornen .... Eheleuten
in der Trattlerbehausung andern Theils, wurde folgender
Vertrag in beysein dem unterschriebenen Zeugen vor-
abredet und geschlossen.

1tens Übernimmt Jacob Glützner, seine zur Wiederbehausten eigen-
thümliche .... Behausung nachmals Badstube vorher
zu einen Stall umgestaltet ist, und zu einen Bauernder
...... sich ein Zimmer und eine Küche befindet, dem Jacob
Harstnig und dessen Eheweib so wie auch ihnen Eheleute
Kindern Jacob und Maria Harstnig auf dessen einen
Einwohnern ganzen Lebens lauen gegen nachstehende
festgesetzte Bedingnissen: als;

2tens Jacob Glützner bedinget sich für diese dem Jacob Harstnig
und dessen Eheweib so wie deren 2 nachfolgenden überlassenen
.... auf ihren Lebens lauen, dass die Elisabeth gebornen
.... so wie ihr Eheman, auf die ihr laut Kaufbrief
.... Obermillstatt am 28ten Dezember 1813 vom
.... gegenwärtige Unterschriebenen im Hirtshaus ......
.... wollen, was auch Elisabeth so wie ihr Eheman ...
gemeinen auf obbenannte Wohnung in Gasthaus nie mehr
....

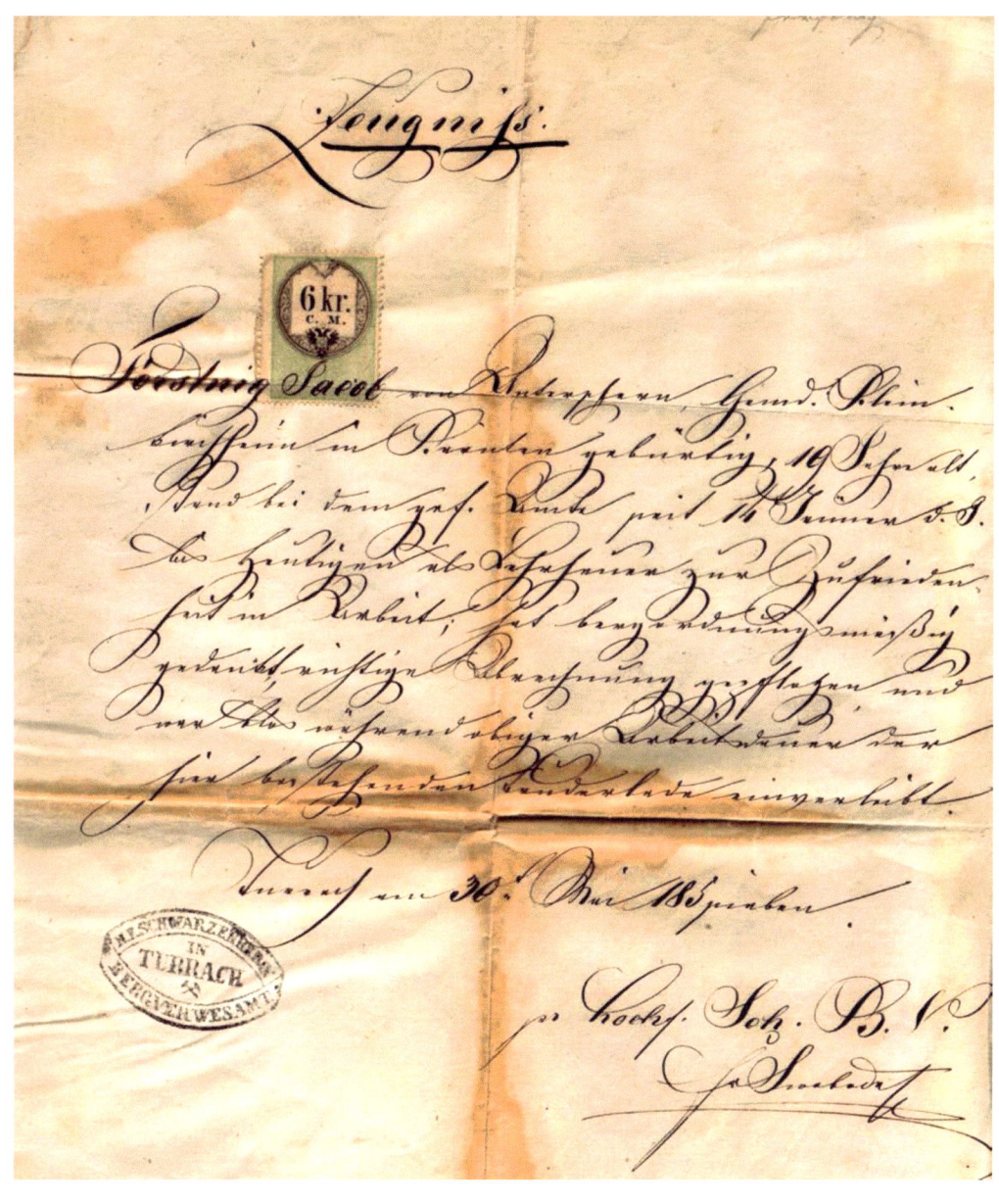

Letter of reference from the *"hochfürstlich Schwarzenbergisches Verwesamt Turrach"*, the regional administrative office of the Princely court in Turrach, for Jakob II Forstnig

Illustration on the opposite page:
Agreement between Jakob Glinzer and Jakob I Forstnig, 6th March 1847

*Carpenters, miners, brewers, soldiers,
gendarmes, lime burners, hauliers, innkeepers,
entrepreneurs, inventors, hoteliers*

THE FORSTNIG FAMILY DYNASTY*

Untertschern around 1920

* Since the present document is the chronicle of the house, only those children who
play a role as successors are listed.

1884–1921   Under the ownership of Jakob II Forstnig.
Jakob II was born in 1837 and was the son of the
carpenter Jakob I Forstnig and his wife Elisabeth,
née Lassnig. Two documents from 1857 and 1858
prove that he was a miner.

On 30th May 1857 the regional administrative office
of the Princely court in Turrach issued him with a
letter of reference confirming his activity as a miner
with prospecting rights for a certain stretch of land.
At this time he took up a post with the mine and hut
administrative department in Radenthein, where he
then worked as an ore sorter, carrier and miner until
the end of September 1858.

How his life and career developed after this remains
unclear, but he was apparently able to earn enough to
buy a building belonging to the Krenhube in Kleinkirch-
heim, which was referred to at the time as a brewing

house, on 21ˢᵗ April 1874. When the contract was drawn up he was described as the owner of the Trattler inn, but this can only refer to the family's right of residence there, since the purchase did not take place until ten years later.

The census in 1880 also recorded the family of Jakob II Forstnig. Their address was given as Kleinkirchheim No. 3 (brewing house). In the household lived Jakob II Forstnig (*17ᵗʰ August 1837) with his wife Anna, née Schleiner (*21ˢᵗ July 1855) and her daughter Anna Schleiner (*26ᵗʰ July 1879).

Since the couple got married in 1880 their daughter, named as Anna Schleiner, must have been the daughter of both of them, although not legitimate.

Jakob II's mother Elisabeth, née Lassnig, is referred to as having the right to live on the farm with them. Jakob II's sister Maria Forstnig (*14ᵗʰ August 1835) also lived in the household, as well as her three children born out of wedlock Elisabeth (*30ᵗʰ October 1858),

Theresia (*13th October 1869) and Maria
(*31st October 1873) as well as Elisabeth's
illegitimate son called Franz (*1st October 1876).

On 24th April 1884, Jakob II sold the brewing
house, which was by now recorded in the land
register as the "Marx property", to the then Mayor
Johann Huber. In return, according to the purchase
agreement of 24th June 1884, he bought the Trattler
inn from its previous owner Albin Stampfer.

In November 1884, the Kleinkirchheim parish
council issued Jakob II Forstnig with a character
reference for the acquisition of a hotel and restaurant
licence. On 10th February 1885, the imperial and
royal finance department issued him with the
certificate entitling him to sell wine and cider.

Probably based on his experience of mining,
Jakob II Forstnig ran a quarry and a lime kiln
on the Woltschnig-Riegel mountain.

Sitting in front: 1st from left Jakob II Forstnig, 3rd from left Anna Forstnig
Standing behind them: 1st from left Katharina Forstnig, 3rd from left Jakob

As well as their daughter Anna mentioned earlier, the couple also had two other children, Jakob (since he did not form part of the succession of the generations or of ownership, we have not used the numbering system for him) and Katharina. Jakob was intended to be the subsequent owner, but he was called up to serve in the First World War, served as a trainee soldier in the 3rd Training Battalion and died on 28th November 1916 in the Campo Pisaro field hospital.

His estate was settled in April 1917, with his parents Jakob II and Anna Forstnig as his heirs. His legacy consisted of one suitcase of clothes, worth 100 crowns, and a bicycle, worth 50 crowns.

Anna and Jakob II.

After the death of his only son, who had been the intended heir, Jakob II Forstnig passed the inn on to his daughter Katharina, who married Johann Hinteregger.

1921–1937   Johann and Katharina Hinteregger (née Forstnig)

Johann and Katharina Hinteregger now took over the ownership of the Trattler property with the transfer agreement of 15th April 1921, subject to the requirement that they take over a form of caretakership for the grandson Jakob III Forstnig, who was born in 1904 and was Katharina's illegitimate son.

They ran the inn on the well-trodden route. As previously, it was mainly waggoners and traders who stopped to eat here and also found modest overnight facilities. Johann and Katharina were recorded in the land register as the owners until the end of 1937.

Katharina and Johann Hinteregger

1937 – 1975   Jakob III. Forstnig

On 30th December 1937 the transfer agreement making Jakob III Forstnig the owner of his parents' guest business was issued. From the Carinthian registers of offices and addresses, it is apparent that he had already taken over the inn shortly after 1930.

In the Second World War he did his military service with the gendarmerie, and during this period his wife Elisabeth took over the running of the inn.

After the War ended, Jakob devoted himself totally to expanding the business, whose profitability was based on different trades just as it had been back in the 17th Century. The main arm of the business was the inn as a place to enjoy summer holidays, with the small farm attached.

There were also the lime kiln and the quarry. In addition, there was a gravel pit and the freight business, which was started in 1945 with an Opel Blitz.

Jakob III. and Elisabeth

Quarry and freight
business

34

In 1950 the inn was extended, and the family also built a new stable. Now that tourism was blossoming again, the inn was doing well and was looked after by Jakob III's wife Elisabeth, while Jakob devoted himself to the other branches of business. Jakob and Elisabeth had five children (Reinhilde, Jakob, Lisbeth, Heimo and Maria).

1975–2010 Jakob IV Forstnig

Jakob IV Forstnig was fully employed in his parents' business as soon as he left business school. He took over the Trattlerhof on 14th November 1975. He devoted himself to the business with great innovation and entrepreneurial spirit, and with strong support from his first wife Elisabeth. Two children were born of this marriage (Jakob and Christiane). His second marriage to Ursula resulted in the birth of Isabella.

The Trattler inn in Untertschern has developed into a four-star category hotel with swimming pool and wellness area and a variety of entertainment facilities. Cattle farming has been replaced by horses.

Trattlerhof
around 1960

Trattlerhof today

The hotel's own stable and paddock offers guests the option of riding in the nearby surroundings or further afield.

A further main pillar gastronomically is the "Einkehr", a quaint restaurant in the centre of Bad Kleinkirchheim, which has four tennis courts, a beach volleyball court and a fishpond with trout and char.

An apartment building and the attached bar "Kir Royal" have also been built in the immediate vicinity of the St Kathrein spa centre.

Jakob IV Forstnig has expanded the sand, gravel and dolomite brick production businesses. In 1985, the Trattlerhof water power station was constructed on the Kirchheimer or Tiefenbach stream. The hotel is still supplied with its own electric power today.

In November 2010, Jakob IV handed over the management of the hotel to his son, who is also called Jakob.

Jakob IV and his invention, a patented food cover

2010 Jakob V Forstnig

Following a comprehensive training at a specialist hotel school, a degree in management sciences and several stays abroad, Jakob V has combined the tradition which stretches back many years with new facilities and innovations: torchlit hikes with horses under the starry skies, relaxing après-ski, "Wine Growers on the Mountain" with wine tastings, or live music by the campfire with mountain lodge romance. The series of dialogues "Impulse on the Mountain" with talks by exceptional personalities has been very well received. Since 2012, guests can have a *dirndl* or *lederhose* made for them during their stay by the resident seamstress and have their shoes customised by the resident shoemaker. In this way old tradition is combined with contemporary luxury.

And now that the farm horses have been given new stalls, the former stables are being turned into a wellness oasis and new accommodation for travellers hungry for experiences.

The Jubilee year 2012 was celebrated with the publication of the Chronicle of the House and the House Legend.

Jakob V. and Birgit Forstnig

The owners of the Trattlerhof since 1520

Ruep Schuster, Georg Rannacher

and Christoph Rannacher 1520 – 30th May 1585

Erasmus Rottenstainer 30th May 1585 – 1592

Afra Rottenstainer 1592 – 14th February 1609

Lamprecht Rottenstainer 14th February 1609 – 1624

Nikolaus Hinteregger 1624 – 1st March 1639

Veith Rottenstainer 1st March 1639 – 16th July 1688

Andre Rottenstainer 16th July 1688 – 23rd June 1729

Kaspar Grayer 23rd June 1729 – 9th February 1748

Christian Wieser 9th February 1748 – 29th March 1751

Jakob Grayer 29th March 1751 – 21st October 1757

Andreas Grayer 21st October 1757 – 29th December 1805

Joseph Grayer 29th December 1805 – ??

Gertraud Hofer ? – ?

Ignaz Grayer ? – 12th May 1821

Christian Laßnig 12th May 1821 – 23rd December 1843

Jakob I Glinzer 23rd December 1843 – 1st November 1847

Johann Lechner 1st November 1847 – 21st November 1849

Michael Hofer 21st November 1849 – 28th November 1854

The bathhouse

Katharina Lechner	28th November 1854 – 21st August 1856
Matthias Stampfer	21st August 1856 – 10th April 1874
Albin Stampfer	10th April 1874 – 29th June 1884
Jakob II Forstnig	29th June 1884 – 15th April 1921
Johann and	
Katharina Hinteregger (née Forstnig)	15th April 1921 – 30th December 1937
Jakob III Forstnig	30th December 1937 – 14th November 1975
Jakob IV Forstnig	14th November 1975 – November 2010
Jakob V Forstnig	November 2010 –

HISTORICAL BACKGROUND

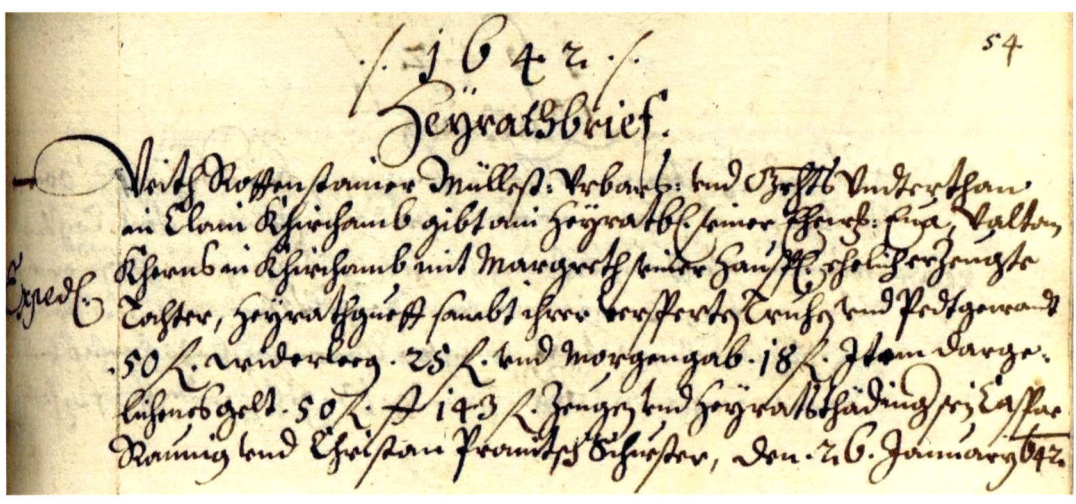

Marriage letter dated 26th January 1642

Until 1848, farmers (apart from freeholders) were answerable to the land owners. This meant that they did indeed possess their farm but only in the sense of being resident on it, not as an owner. The landlord (nobility, monastery, church or parish) reserved the right to make virtually all the decisions in terms of rights of ownership. In the early Middle Ages the landlords' estates were managed from central farms, but later this changed to the running of individual farms. The farmers were allocated small farms which were originally provided with cattle and all the equipment by the landlords. The farmers who were not free were obliged to pay levies, consisting of the fruits of their fields, the profits from raising their cattle and performing work in person on the landlords' dairy farms.

Over time the conditions for the farmers were relaxed. Two rights of ownership developed for farmers, *Freistiftgerechtigkeit* and the right to buy. The lesser form – the *Freistiftrecht* – offered farmers very little scope for development. Every change required the consent of the landlord and there was no right of inheritance. "Owning" a farm under these terms meant that the farmer could be removed at any time. This was only rarely the case in practice, but it could actually happen if the farm was managed badly.

The landlords, who were reliant on the results of their farms, naturally endeavoured to keep the hard-working farmers. Thus over time a right of inheritance developed which, as many examples show, even allowed women to inherit the farms.

As the second form of ownership, the right of purchase allowed a farmer to freely inherit, exchange or sell his estate. He too was still a subject with all the levies this involved, but he could dispose much more freely what he owned. In all cases of the transfer of ownership, so-called *"Ehrungsbriefe"* (letters of tribute) were issued. The fee payable for this was referred to as *"Ehrung"* (tribute) and was usually around ten percent of the value of the property.

These transfers were registered in the landlords' tribute books. In addition, rental rolls or registers of tributes were kept, in which the annual levies were recorded. The right to buy could itself be bought, and many farmers used this to gain at least a small portion of independence.

In 1848 an event occurred which was of great significance for farming people: the abolition of their subservience, the dissolution of the manorial (landlord) system and the subsequent agrarian reform.

On 7th September 1848 Emperor Ferdinand declared subservience abolished and ordered that land should be released in return for a small recompense, and in some cases for no payment at all. In this way farmers really became owners of their property.

The ordinance in this respect for the principality of Carinthia was issued on 11th September 1848, and two years later the enforcement of the agrarian reform started. The farmers themselves had to pay one third of 20 times the annual interest to their landlords as a redemption sum, and this could be paid in cash or in three annual instalments.

It took a long time to estimate the interest payable in kind and issue the exoneration certificates. Commissioners travelled the land and undertook the calculations, so it was a number of years before the farmers who were now free had the exoneration certificates in respect of their land in their hands.

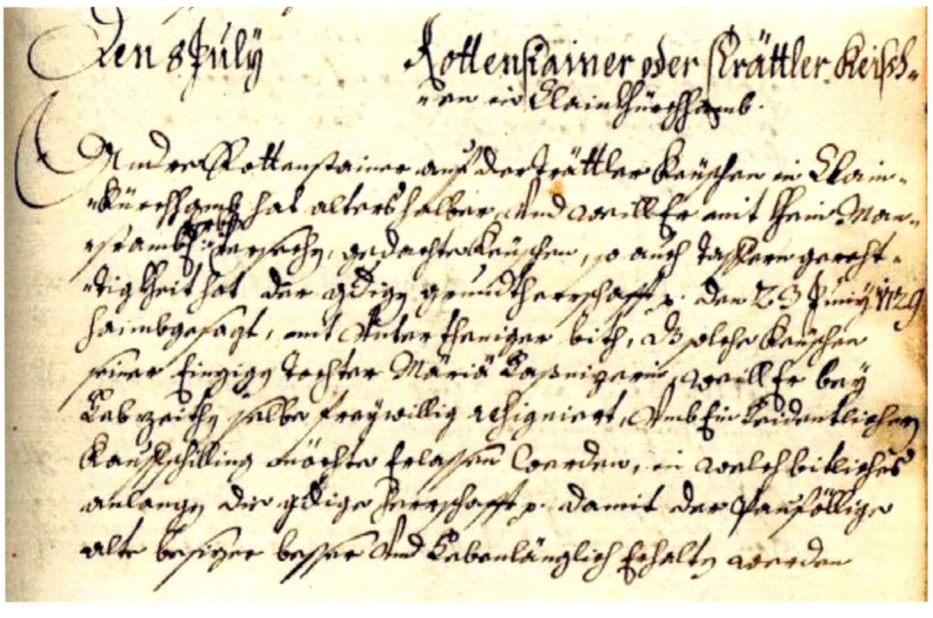

8th July 1729 Maria Lassnitzer and Kaspar Grayer

werden möchte, auch mitleiden nach gewilliget, und
dieser Rauschen ihr Maria Sazwignerin auf fl 200 auf
ihr Lebenlang frauchtlich verschafft, dem welchen Antheil-
ling doch dem Alten per modum Allmosind 17 Kazn,
gehalten worden, dessen Zeugen gewest Hr Ignatig
... Landrichter in ..., Frang ... ...
... allda, Hans Moser Müllethanich, und
Mathes ... Hl pfarrmesl Hn ... ...
... Weil aber bey aufrichtung des Inven-
tary befunden worden, als das schulden das Vermögen
mehr dann Alle 200 fl überschweng, Und welchen die Wittwe
Maria zu bezahlen, Und auch zu haben Hat, ihr gedachte
Rauschen ihr nächsten Vatter Vatter in Krag Voabee-
knappen Cedirt; doch mit dem beding, das er neben
bezahlung des obbemelten Rauschschilling Und Lebenläng-
licher Anbehaltung ihrer Alten Mutter, auch 100 fl
denen Creditorib bey ... ...; welchab er Vatter in
Krag alles gebräuglich zu halten, Und zu folgnahn der
... auch bey gediger ... Und Freundschaft
... fl 4 Diggathen in gold abgebrochen. Zeugen
dessen seind Frang ..., Hans Moser zu bey.
Und Hans Franz ... Und ... in ver
... bey ...

Source: Joachim Eichert, Bäuerliches Besitzrecht in früherer Zeit,
KLM Heft 9/10, 1995, page 112

EINKEHR

The Einkehr, the mountain lodge restaurant in the Bad Kleinkirchheim valley, has lots of good things on offer for epicures, gourmets, fans of Carinthian cooking and people with a sweet tooth:

- Cosy dining rooms and a sunny terrace
- Regional delicacies, dishes, pizza
- Homemade pastries
- Mulled wine parties by the campfire
- Family celebrations, parties and weddings
- Fishpond with trout and char
- 4 tennis courts and a beach volleyball court
- 2x weekly live music
- Wine tastings and taster menus
- Hot food served every day from 11.00 to 22.00

Table reservations on 04240/8114

Einkehr
The mountain lodge restaurant in the valley
Teichstraße 7
9546 Bad Kleinkirchheim
Carinthia • Austria
Phone: +43 (0)4240 / 8114
einkehr@trattlerhof.at
www.trattlers-einkehr.at

TRATTLERHOF
★★★★

Join us
in celebrating
370 years
of hospitality!

The TRATTLERHOF is in the centre of Bad Kleinkirchheim – the famous holiday town in the alpine heart of Carinthia. A holiday at the TRATTLERHOF is an experience for all the family, the romantically minded or simply people looking for an escape from everyday life.

The Forstnig family • Gegendtalerweg 1 • 9546 Bad Kleinkirchheim • Carinthia • Austria
Phone: +43 (0) 4240 / 8172 • Fax: +43 (0) 4240 / 8124 • hotel@trattlerhof.at

www.trattlerhof.at

Already published
in the Trattlerhof series:

Der Trattlerhof und seine Geschichte (Chronik des Hauses)
ISBN 9 783848205004

The Trattlerhof and its History (The Chronicle of the House)
ISBN 9 783848266791

Il Trattlerhof e la sua storia (Cronaca della casa)
ISBN 9 783848211029

Das Hofmärchen vom Schwarzen Pferdle
ISBN 9 783848204915

The House Legend of the Black Horse
ISBN 9 783848266562

La favola del cavallino nero
ISBN 9 783848204960

Das Märchenmalbuch/Coloring Book
ISBN 9 783848204991